Ripples to Waves

Sunny Anahata

BookLeaf Publishing
India | USA | UK

Presentation by *BookLeaf Publishing*

Web: www.bookleafpub.com

E-mail: info@bookleafpub.com

ISBN: 9789358368239

First edition 2023

The Unknown

I hold my breath
   and face toward the sun
Counting the seconds left
   until winter is done
Remembering that losses are
   simply reminders I've won
I greet myself at the gates
   of the great unknown

I give in to breaking down
   and raising my voice

Life carries such a beautiful way
   of giving us choice

The Craftsman with every tool
   both creates and destroys

He calls me to break down walls
   then sing songs to rejoice

The ground is warm and alive
   and so am I
I release my burdens
   to the setting sky

The birds are singing
  and I know why
They leapt off branches
  to learn to fly

Chronicles of a Wounded Healer

check myself
check my time
is there reason?
is there rhyme?
take it slow
and find the flow
that brings the glow up with the climb
steady onward
more to find
steady inward
through the mind
to the body
carbon copy
melt like Dali
and align
heed the signs
to the nines
feel the light
and how it shines
spark the wisdom
in the silence of the gifts
from the Divine
but with light
darkness moves

shadows waiting
as they do
not to repel me
but to tell me
every way I can improve
as above
so below
there is always room to grow
from what I see and I perceive
and everything I've come to know
fight or flee
isn't me
not who I came here to be
wretched history
karmic mystery
balance from insanity
gave them power
took it back
found abundance
in the lack
if creation isn't mine
then I'm a train that's lost its track
even if I'm on one leg
even if my nerves are tired
even if the static comes to fry me up
I won't retire
what transpired
needs released
grounding now to find my feet

I can stand
on my own land
and find direction on my street
it's my path
always learning
always teaching
seasons turning
birth, destroy, renew, allow
and keep the candle always burning
speak when open
be as love
as below, so above
listen closely
to the spirit
and the consequence thereof
choices, they are limitless
I know I align with this
so I'll keep growing
infinite
and seal each wound up with a kiss

Blue

It started with Blue
and permeated the entirety of my being

Such a rhapsody in Blue

As the pulse of the Nile
it swims between hemispheres
    eroding mundane error
    enticing words unspoken
    flooding my core in an orgasmic wave

The ocean...
She rings Freedom

So reflective a mirror

An hourglass raining salted years
down my face
now through an emerald smile

I find myself immersed
thanking the windows of You
    that shed Light
        on a Path worth foreseeing

It started with Blue

Feathers

Feathers glide down
onto open sunlit patches of Earth -

The soil ever eager
to receive fallen matter to rebirth.

Birds still carry on,
singing songs overhead, acquiescing:

"If we're all here to Be,
there's no danger in not second guessing.

My dear, let the River
cut into your mountains and cool them,

And if vows to your Spirit are broken,
I pray that you renew them.

Let sunshine wash through you,
bring Light to the deepest of caverns,

Unwind and release you,
restore you, and refill your lanterns."

Such beauty before us,
laid out like the seeds left in Eden.

Creator created,
it's time to stop seeking and receive them.

Gifts will unfold,
Hearts will armor with gold:
It is written.

As feathers reclaimed
build us wings once again,
We are forgiven.

Here and Now

Past
Unconscious
Wayward stalking
In the mindless thinking, talking
Uses of excuses
As to why there is no forward walking

Treadmills of insanity
A plague amongst humanity
An arbitrary loss of presence
Carried out in vanity
By holding onto chains that bind us
Illusory frames that blind us
From the Power we all breathe
In moments that, in Truth, remind us

Growth is paramount and vital
Reach beyond the root survival
To the places
That Light spaces in the heart
Release entitled absence
From the calling onward
Slough off these old stories
Over-heard and over-spoken
Homeward

Extricate limits
Revival in the DNA
Non-dual in the "we" and "they"
Approval
To birth freedom through renewal

Every fear may be transmuted
If it's stripped of every mystery
That withheld it from the surface
And got trapped somewhere in history

Let the One that gifts us wings
Rectify all need for things
That pull us backward
Bring us balance
In a harmony that sings
For Here and Now
And nothing less
With loving hands
Relieving stress
And growing seeds
Where once infertile
And deserted from our needs

For there is only ever Now
Reception welcome
Visions clear
With disillusionment and confidence
To know our purpose Here

Silence

In the stillness
In the absence of creation
Shadows forming
With reminders of a light within
So gracious and so warming
Flood the channels
Drench the atmosphere in candor
I-and-I-and-
I Am taken
By the waves that salt my skin
And leave it dampened
Under sunsets
Under prisms that sing stories for reflections
Tides come in and tides ebb out
Like breath of water
Resurrections
Chapters closing
Place a bookmark
And surrender to the senses
Drop the oars
And float the ripples
Til the next chapter commences

Alchemy

If all I have left is
  the skin on my bones,
This heart in my chest,
  and this light of my own -
No shiny sound objects,
  no oils and no stones -
No chimes, bells, or herbals
  for guarding my home -
No potions and no spells
  for erasing exes -
No salt, sage or incense
  for cleansing the exits -
Just my barefooted prowess
  and rich solar plexus,
Let these hands be enough
  to heal what disconnects us.

Phoenix

When the orchard grows a virus
Grab the pen and the papyrus
Write it out of history
Then hand it over to Osiris
If the knowledge was forbidden
No one here would be forgiven
Time would cease
With no more chances
To remember what's inside us
Let the Universe provide us
Let the stars move to collide us
Bite the apple
And ignore the voices that seek to divide us
Storm the gates and break the silence
Break the chains
And end the violence
Elevate
And co create
And end the hate
And reunite us
Leave the fear
Erase the -itis
Apple of my eye
Sweet iris
Bloom with me

And count to three
And let the flame rise to ignite us

Seasons of a Witch

One:

I am autumn
tears of the gods
drop leaves and rooves
strong winds steal branches
impending decay on the horizon
light lessening
harvested and shut down
dreary but colorful
chilling yet soothing
wise, unpredictable
and fallen

Two:

I am winter
frozen, I died off
a daunting season of ice
and stillness within
cracking and drying
preserving
self-reliance in survival
incidental hibernation
sickness defaulted
often alone

Three:

I am a long winter
nights endless
withdrawn
commanding, rigid
armored and distant
breaking just through the surface
no more, no less
and hardened
just enough room for repair
and for none to enter

Four:

I am spring
pollinating in layers
fertile with potential
flowing in pastel and rainstorms
resurging, rebirthing and growing
constructive, productive
airy and welcome
and warming
renewed soil
rendered Earth for rooting
and seeding as I go

Five:

I am summer
healing sunshine
abundant
fruit-bearing
shades of red-orange linger
dawn stirs all awakening
stunning in green
a provisioner of play
exploration
resplendent congregation
a magnet for smiles
an instiller of refill
balancing extreme temperament
and a reminder
to see nature fully
through all elements
and breathe

Hieros Gamos

Make mistakes
Pump your brakes
Learn the lesson and give thanks
Cue the sanskrit
Pull the hands in
Kundalini
Namaste
Chrism rising
Charm the snakes
Dance the Earth
Until it quakes
Focus on the hocus pocus
Of the magic Spirit makes

Set your bounds
And break their rules
And reprogram the music
Heart is open
Soul renewed
So use it now, or lose it
Mother Gaia
Wide awake
For justice and rebirthing
Calling all Her babies Home
Reminding us we're worthy

Breathe it in
Ignite the skin
And cleanse your sin
And come to win
Reclaim your power
Final hour
Manipura shine and spin
Let Muladhara take your sorrow
Carry you into tomorrow
Svadisthana
Wake and play
And orchestrate the voice within

The choice within is now awakened   Guiding
you to green and blue
This is where you now prepare
To share the Home that's calling you Repair the
Heart
Speak the Truth
Give up anything for sooth
Stabilize and equalize
And let it rise up from the root

Sixth arrival
Frankincense
Clarity is Heaven sent
Indigo
We gather close

Reintegrate in sacrament
Sky and Earth
Mind, Body, Soul
The Father, Son and Holy Ghost
We drink the Water
Fill our cups
And consecrate our common goal

Sahasrara
Beacon rise
Unify and light the skies
Divination
Healing station
Frequencies that harmonize
Let it be
So it is
Humble seekers bearing gifts
The time is near
Have no fear
Shiva paved the way for this

Shakti
Shanti virabhadrasana
Gilded
Skilled with autonomic armor
Eyes shut
Sun lit
Ajna in a sauna
Do no harm

Take no shit
Anahata honor

Aurora

Uproot her with your treasure maps
Breathe her sails out
Bridge the gaps

Westbound songbird lifts her nest
For restitution
Strong and blessed

Paint her under fluid skies
Her star-kissed skin
Your sandstone eyes

Wash her with your greens and blues
Immersive Love
Enchanted hues

Lift the corners of her lips
Embellish her
With fingertips

Of fiddleheads and peony
And blissful
Hillside majesty

Unroll her in your fertile soil
Revitalized
By blood and toil

Her heart and vision unified
On healing lands
As prophesied

Release

Peaceful Warrior
Cease this fight
Let the Left
Receive the Right

Build the bridges
Drop the sword
Justice yearned for
Grace implored

Thank the lesson
Pay respect
Apologize
Reconnect

Kiss the paper
Burn the pain
Live through Love
Complete again

Surrender

Whispers in the boundless wind,
"Love, leave behind this aftertaste."

Chills roll to the tip of my tongue.
I spit each binding thought out in haste.

The language of time rings louder still,
"Surrender, darling...

Let it go."

Fleeting minutes to infinite hours,
"In comforted darkness, all things grow."

An empty vessel is an open channel
For propagation of faith, unshakeable.

Standing flush with this cliffside,
I ask now for a Heart unbreakable.

Wanderlust serves its purpose
For the mind that wonders deeper,

But stretch me to my greatest wingspan;

Trust the wind to catch this leaper.

Sinking to increased potential,
I draw this arrow back, and smile.

Tension mounts before release...

Then, I jump

               to fly awhile.

I trust the current
    and myself
And every step that brought me here.

And so, in flight, I whisper back,

"Hello, Love.

    Goodbye, fear."

The Giver

a bottomless well
of passion and mystical flow
sweet Giver
surrendering and submitting
without reservation
without hesitation
with grace and gentility
to the motion
of her lover's silent echoes

so immersed
this Giver
with the eyes to see
and the heart to know
his unspoken words

his very existence
reason alone
to deepen her awareness
of their sharpest points
and their smoothest edges
exponentiating her desires
to embrace him
to amaze him
to unlock him

in unforeseen, yet intentional moments
of a heightened sensation
that freezes thought and time
and entrances the body
in a restorative current
of unchained harmony
where gravity is lost
where Oneness is found
where sacrum meets the heart
where the Giver
 merges with her greatest Love

Remembrance

resurrection child
braided in the sacred womb
unravels itself

feet rooted in stars
native to constellations
children of the sky

violet-washed halos
fruits of the vine spread with tact
tasting the vision

The New Story

Said the stars,
"Come as you are,"
with the scars of time unraveled
on roads not often traveled
Clay of crimson, none graveled
Feet stained with wayward history
of these deepening channels
Solution in the mystery
Firelight of the candles
So dismantle the old views
Absorb each lesson gifted
The time it took to sift it
is relative to the mystic
For all that was encrypted
shall find the heart and lift it
to feathers on the scales
in the temples we live in
The Father, our breath expanded
The Mother is where we landed
Such trial and error
to receive the callings we're handed
We are branded with a truth
that only asks that we share it
And to bring in the new story
to the children who inherit

Limitless

vibration
 and sensation
  and creation
   are synonymous
the words you speak
 the life you seek
  they may be seen anomalous
but you came here
 to be the change
  that breaks the chains
   on consciousness
    to upgrade your environment
     to sing through the monotonous
so heal and share
 and give and praise
  and uninvite the ominous
   and find things to be thankful for
rebirth yourself autonomous
 and stretch the limitations set
devote yourself like Artemis
 and dispel needless conflict
  in a way that is magnanimous
though through the darkness
 serpent fangs may leave you
  feeling venomous

releasing poison
 without bleeding out
  is now the emphasis
a call to one
 a call to all
  a call to heed the messages
remembrance of your purpose here
 your joy
  your love
   your genesis
that which you feel
 becomes what's real
  and you secure your premises
nobody else will do it for you
 simplify your edifice
  and build it up on solid ground
   and monitor the entrances
    and raise your flag
     and light your windows
      knowing you are limitless

Revival

Children of the macrocosmic implosion
grow the seeds
of bioluminescent oxytocin
Symbiotic by design
The prana and the potion
That dihydrogen monoxide flow
of all word spoken
Existential Kintsugi
Thaw out every heart frozen
and gild the cracks
in every single circle unbroken
Those chosen
Those awoken here
to serve in Devotion
with a motion like the ocean
Salt of Earth for the wounds that will open
We, the tides that choose to rise
Fly the skies
and open eyes
We're the lanterns on the darkest paths
Compasses that guide
So we stay loyal to the mission
Seek absolution of division
Bring the North, the South,
the East, the West

a centralized vision
Write the revision
It's vital
A microcosmic revival
Let the ripples make the waves
that lift us out of survival
DIY EMF from inside you
Evergreen that exhales to ignite you
Eat the fruits of the Spirit that light you
and watch the Universe expand to provide you

Anahata

Between the Love that was lost
and the Love that was asked for
There's a madness on the path
and it quakes with a thirst to know more

In the silence, I sit
with connection to all that is pure
A creation that stirs up release
and gives space for the cure

There's no need to ask why
All the answers were already there
tangible to digging hands
and a mind seeking how to repair

What was lost can be found
Keep me open with eyes indigo
and a bridge through the heart
over waters that endlessly flow

Guide me through every lesson
in every reflection, I pray,
with a knowledge that births
light in darkness to show me the way

Non-Attachment

Artificial lighting
Societal suggestion
Frequencies emitted
For vacuous ingestion

A phantom hierarchy
Equality obscured
With such relentless longing
Such suffering endured

A paper-worth entrapment
Insatiable collection
A thirst for different sameness
But need for real connection

Insanity in masses
Collective loss of purpose
The world now beckons many
To heal to come to service

Release fearful attachment
Release desire for grandeur
Release approvals yearned for
Cease chasing every answer

Materials don't matter
We outweigh every output
Immeasurable value
A call to shift our outlook

Beyond the threat of judgment
Beyond the blue light sirens
Beyond egoic structure
Beyond pre-programmed violence

Beyond the shallow romance
And back to conscious content
Revisiting the I Am
Reactive to respondent

To leave all lack behind us
Find gratitude with reason
Eradicate identity
Remember our completion

So pure, the poor in spirit
Blessing freely without chains
For once our time is up here
Just Love is what remains

Found in Translation

Your "tomayto", my "tomahto":
Dhanvantari or Apollo.
If the medicine
is what we can believe in,
we will swallow.
There's no law,
there's no jury,
nor a doctrine,
nor your fury
that can block the path that
Spirit paves for each of us to follow.
Know the ledge,
but feel the language.
Know there's many ways to say this.
Know that Themis, Durga, Ishtar, Baldr
all have the same address.
It's the message,
word incarnate -
Symbolism of the karmic
and the dharmic -
Does no harm,
but takes no shit
and guides the arm
that grabs the ankh from our Creator
through the fabric of our nature

and gives Isis proper insight
to align us with our Maker.
Through the roots of Pachamama
and the dance of sister Shakti
and the lions from the Lyran nations
showing us our calling:
Shadows falling,
Christos rising,
Atman stirring what's inside and,
so aligning,
Anahata beckons Ra to come igniting,
shining light and giving guidance.
Find the healing in the violence,
and unite us
in a truth that burns the walls down
that divide us.
Sing the hymns of integration,
reach the Heart of every nation,
and dispel the pull to worship
one dogmatic inclination,
for the Truth is
we are One here.
We have much to overcome here,
and the way-showers are rising
to show that which must be done here.
Through the dark into the light,
whatever your mode of flight,
your deitic inspiration
or experiential plight,

find your medicine and use it.
Learn it, so you don't misuse it,
and give thanks to every ancestor
that brought you here to choose it.
You're the music, you're the lyric,
the composer is your spirit,
And the choir of angels sings
where you can hear it,
so don't fear it.
Though your path is not my own,
there's no right way set in stone,
but for loving one another
as we walk each other Home.

www.ingramcontent.com/pod-product-compliance
Lightning Source LLC
LaVergne TN
LVHW051240200726

843510LV00011B/1629